and
yet–

here
you
are

EILEEN LAMB

**THOUGHT
CATALOG**
Books

THOUGHTCATALOG.COM

THOUGHT CATALOG Books

Published by Thought Catalog Books, an imprint of Thought Catalog, a digital magazine owned and operated by The Thought & Expression Co. Inc., an independent media organization founded in 2010 and based in the United States of America. For stocking inquiries, contact stockists@shopcatalog.com.

Produced by Chris Lavergne and Noelle Beams
Art direction and design by KJ Parish
Creative editorial direction by Brianna Wiest
Circulation management by Isidoros Karamitopoulos

thoughtcatalog.com | shopcatalog.com

First Edition, Limited Edition Print
Printed in the United States of America

ISBN 978-1-949759-91-4

INTRODUCTION

How do you comfort someone whose worst fear has just become a reality? How do you navigate the loss of the person you vowed forever to? Can the unforgivable ever find forgiveness?

As I entered the nightmarish phase of my life, I wrestled with conflicting thoughts. There were moments I doubted my sanity—writing one thing one day and the complete opposite the next. However, I've realized I'm not losing my mind; I'm just going through something I hope others never endure. The contradiction within me isn't madness; it's the turmoil between heart and head. We never grow if we never question ourselves or change our minds.

Whatever you're going through, you will survive it. I promise you. Because what you're experiencing isn't unique, countless others have known heartache, fear, and failure. But only a fraction dare to share their deepest struggles. We may feel alone, but that isolation only persists because people fear vulnerability.

As you read my words, you may find yourself conflicted. One day, page 8 resonates; the next, page 15. That's the beauty of life—we're constantly evolving.

What feels true one moment may shift the next, and that's okay.

I'm not here to stir you in a specific direction—I'm here to walk alongside you as you navigate life's ups and downs. Through these pages, I want you to know that I get it. I get *you*.

This book is a raw glimpse into the mind of someone who confronted her greatest fear and emerged stronger.

There's no end to this story—I'm still writing it.

Dear heart,

I'm sorry for not always protecting you. I apologize for leaving you in the hands of those who couldn't handle you and for not consistently choosing you. I regret being reckless and placing hope above rational thoughts, exposing you to unnecessary pain.

I take full responsibility for this. Please allow me to put your pieces back together. We can do it. I've learned from my mistakes how to care for and protect you. I understand your needs now.

Comfort and the fear of loneliness aren't worth risking another betrayal. I've learned that I won't be plagued by constant self-doubt when love is right.

You and I share the longest relationship and I'm committed to treating you better 'til death do us part.

Please forgive me.

There are few things as agonizing as losing someone you believed would be a permanent part of your life. At least, that's the sentiment in those moments.

That's what it feels like when your days and nights don't seem to end and life appears devoid of happiness. That's what it feels like, then. I stress *then* because when sadness clouds your perspective, it's challenging to see that pain is temporary. I assure you, it won't always feel like someone is wrenching your heart from your chest. The darkness won't persist indefinitely. Enduring the ache of losing someone you never thought you'd lose requires courage. Yes, it's going to hurt, but not forever.

Even if the chaos of the moment obscures it, each passing day brings you closer to a new beginning. Eventually, you'll be able to reflect on the past and appreciate the lessons it taught you.

I wish I had understood sooner that even the most profound love requires work.

It's not just about finding your person and waiting for life to breeze by as effortlessly as those initial moments.

See, love doesn't shield you from disagreements and misunderstandings. It doesn't guarantee a perpetual flutter in your stomach. Love doesn't mean you'll never get sick of going through the motions together.

Love doesn't prevent life from getting complicated.

Love is about commitment.

When love becomes challenging, you have a choice:

Take the easy way out and walk away
or
Stand together and fight.

Sometimes, we stay for the wrong reasons. Maybe we fear becoming another statistic in divorce databases. Perhaps comfort outweighs our self-esteem. Or the idea of being physically alone is scarier than enduring emotional loneliness with someone. Sometimes, we stay for the sake of others or because we're too exhausted for such a significant change. Other times, we wait, hoping the storm will pass.

We choose to stay for many reasons, but often, they're just excuses rooted in a fear of change. When we remain despite having our hearts broken by another human being, no justification is enough to make it worthwhile.

Leaving behind something you thought would last forever is one of life's harshest experiences. But be kind to yourself; don't waste time with those who don't know how to handle your heart with care.

When you're the girl who overthinks, every interaction, every glance, and every subtle gesture becomes a reflection of your own thoughts and fears.

When you're the girl who overthinks, you replay conversations in your mind before they even take place, thinking through responses to make sure you're prepared for any outcome. It becomes a coping mechanism—a way to deal with the unpredictable.

When you're the girl who overthinks, you master the art of imagining the worst-case scenario to protect yourself from disappointment. It's not that you're pessimistic by nature but rather that you've learned to protect yourself from the ache of unmet expectations.

When you're the girl who overthinks, you struggle looking into people's eyes, afraid they'll be able to see right through you. You fear they'd be able to see those insecurities you work so hard to hide.

When you're the girl who overthinks, every aspect of life can feel like a constant struggle against your own mind. Simple decisions become big decisions, where your mind plays out endless possibilities and consequences.

When you're the girl who overthinks, relationships can be especially challenging. You find yourself dissecting every word and action of your partner, searching for hidden meanings behind every word.

When you're the girl who overthinks, self-doubt is with you every step of the way. You second-guess every choice you make, wondering if it's right. Your inner critic never seems to quiet down and constantly reminds you of every time you failed before.

When you're the girl who overthinks, you struggle to fall asleep. Your mind is always racing with thoughts, replaying conversations and scenarios from years ago that could have gone differently.

When you're the girl who overthinks, social situations become a mountain to climb. You're hyper-aware of every word you say and every move you make. You fear rejection and struggle to let your guard down and be yourself, constantly worried about how others perceive you.

But the girl who overthinks is also the most empathetic and understanding friend. She is in tune with how others are feeling and always the first to offer support and guidance in ways others may be unable to.

If you're the girl who overthinks, remember that while being an overthinker may feel like a constant battle, it proves your strength. You have to work twice as hard at doing things most people take for granted. And that, my friend, is impressive.

when you
feel like all
hope is lost,

remember
that old
volcanoes,
once deemed
dormant,
have erupted
again.

Forgiving an affair is one of the
hardest things you'll ever do.

It's looking at him and wondering
if he's thinking about her.

It's being suspicious when his boss
asks him to work overtime.

It's doubting that his friend Jack
actually exists. Is it Jennifer?

It's wanting to believe him with all your heart
but being hit by rational thinking every
time something unexpected comes up.

It's seeing him happy and wondering if it's
because he secretly saw her at the grocery store.

Forgiving is the bravest thing you
can do and the craziest too.

It's screaming, "I'm hurting but I'm willing to
risk my heart being shattered into a million
pieces *again* to give us the chance we deserve."

Forgiving takes work and, honestly, naivety.

Forgiving takes two people who choose
to fight where most people have decided
to give up, often rightfully so.

this
bedroom,
once a
sanctuary
for our love,

is now a
graveyard
of what we
once had.

You can't force destiny. Just because your best friend found love in her twenties doesn't mean that's what's in the cards for you.

What if everything you're going through was preparing you to find the love of your life in your 40s? What if the best is yet to come? What if everything you've ever dreamed of will happen on a timeline different from what you hoped? What if it's never too late? What if the universe has been orchestrating a masterpiece in your life, with each twist and turn leading you closer to a love that surpasses your wildest dreams?

Every heartache, challenge, and moment of doubt paves the way for something better than you ever imagined. Perhaps the universe is simply aligning the stars, preparing to deliver a love that exceeds your expectations. And who's to say that this love won't arrive precisely when you're ready to receive it, when your heart is open, and your mind has finally been able to let go of past heartache?

Enjoy the present day even if it's hard, knowing that every experience and challenge shapes you into the person you were always meant to be.

And remember, love knows no limits of time or age. Whether you're in your twenties, thirties, forties, or beyond, the possibility of finding true love is ever-present. Sometimes, you just have to trust that things are happening exactly as they should.

sometimes,
it takes a
little longer
for your heart
to understand
what your
head has
always
known.

In the grand theater of life, there's never a perfect moment. I hope you don't wait too long before making a decision. It's easy to convince yourself it's the wrong timing. It's easy to get caught up in "just one more day," but time is precious, and you won't be on this earth forever.

Imagine where you'd be if you had decided a year ago. Don't let the fear of uncertainty paralyze you. Don't allow the comfort of familiarity to force you into waiting. Every moment spent waiting is a moment lost—a chance forfeited, a possibility left unexplored.

I hope you think of the choices you wish you had made ten years ago and use those as a guide to help you today so that in ten years, you won't regret your actions or lack thereof.

We often get stuck in relationships that suck the life out of us. We cling to what's familiar, convincing ourselves that tomorrow will bring change, that somehow the pain will ease, and happiness will get back into our lives.

But deep down, we know the truth. Life's too short to settle for anything less than real connection, the kind that lights up our souls and makes us feel alive.

You got this.

do
the
things
that
scare
you.

Sometimes, when we're feeling down, all we truly need is someone who gets it. Not someone who tries to fix the problem but someone who acknowledges that, yes, life can be tough. We want to feel like our struggles aren't being dismissed but instead met with empathy and support. We're not necessarily seeking solutions; we just want to feel understood in our struggles. We long for that understanding–a simple recognition that someone else understands it, that we're not alone.

Make room in your heart for someone who chooses you every single day, not just when it's easy or convenient but also when your world is falling apart. Make room for the kind of person who shows up, not because they have to but because they want to.

Make space for someone who stands by your side through the highs and the lows. Someone who doesn't just talk the talk but walks the walk. Someone who proves their love to you through their actions day in and day out.

In a world that's constantly changing, where people come and go, make room for someone who stays— someone who builds their home in your heart and accepts you exactly as you are.

I know it's not easy to tear down your walls and let another human being into the deepest parts of your being, especially after the last one broke your heart. But trust me, it's worth it. Don't shut yourself off.

You'll wake up one day and what used to feel so heavy won't anymore. Everything will still echo with reminders of them, but rather than being overwhelmed with sadness, you'll feel a sense of acceptance. Memories will wash over you, yet instead of falling apart like you used to, you'll feel oddly at peace.

It may seem unattainable right now but just because you can't see it doesn't mean it's not there. Don't let temporary sadness permanently cloud your mind.

When strength
becomes your only option,
you'll discover it was
always within you.
You simply never had the
opportunity to let it shine.

Walking away from a changing relationship is daunting. It's a fight you have to win against yourself—against the part of you that's still entangled in the past and can't cease obsessing over what it used to be like.

It's remembering the daily phone talks, struggling to understand why the line is now silent. It's missing them so much. Too much. It's remembering those inside jokes that could turn your day around and wondering if you'll ever experience that connection again. And above all, it's an overwhelming feeling of sadness over those once precious moments that are now in the past.

But it's also sensing them slipping away, hoping it's just a phase—a rite of passage in the ups and downs of a typical relationship. It's clinging to the belief that things can be good again. Not today, but someday. Maybe, hopefully—who knows?

It's longing for them to open up. It's hoping you're imagining things despite that nagging suspicion that you're not. It's seeing them distance themselves as a sign of time passing by.

And finally, it's accepting that love is indeed gone while trying to fill a void that seems infinite.

It's all of these things and more, so that's why you can't *just* walk away without it ripping your heart apart. Be gentle with yourself as you navigate this in-between stage.

People change, relationships evolve, and love transforms. Accepting this truth is challenging; no manual guides you through this journey. It's difficult to accept that those who once brought you the most joy can gradually fade away, slowly diminishing before your eyes.

You're left empty, a void that is not quick to refill. Just know that you did nothing wrong by trying. It's heartbreaking when things change but that doesn't mean it's your fault. Don't cling too tightly to a one-sided structure—eventually, you'll be completely upside-down.

The bravest thing you've ever done was choosing to stay when every logical part of your being urged you to throw in the towel.

I don't care if it failed or succeeded—staying was brave.

You fought for what you believed in. That's more than many can say.

Be proud of yourself.

The in-between stage is painful.

It's a dance between what your
heart wants and what your
head tries to convince you of.

I know you're only staying because the fear of waking up in the middle of the bed is paralyzing.

I know you dread being left alone with your thoughts, terrified of confronting the emptiness within.

I know you wonder if you have it in you to survive a fresh start and start all over again.

But I also know that your anxiety isn't telling you that what you're so worried about will soon become something you will cherish more than anything. Indeed, those moments of solitude you are so afraid of are slowly teaching you the purest form of love: self-love.

Soon, you'll actually enjoy being alone.

sometimes,
people come
to you not
because they
want a
solution
but because
they want
someone
to listen
to them.

She waited forever for an apology, yearning to hear some semblance of remorse. She hoped for him to understand how deeply his actions had wounded her, craving an understanding of the consequences.

She held onto hope as if it were her only lifeline, wishing that an apology could take away her pain. But all she received was a deafening silence.

He wasn't sorry for the pain he caused her.

He was sorry he got caught.

Sometimes, the right decision hurts.
It doesn't matter how obvious the
right choice seems to everyone else.
They're not the ones living your
life. Listen to people's advice but
don't let it speak over your heart.

you
deserve
more
than
what
you
think
you
want.

May life bring friends into your path who are meant to stay.

I hope you find people who don't solely call you when they want to go out but people who will make you understand the true meaning of the word "friend."

I hope life connects you with someone who will stand by your side through thick and thin.

I hope you meet the person you can call day and night with fearless conviction they will pick up the phone.

I hope you find someone who will lend you their shoulder to cry on and their hand to hold when the weight of the world is too heavy to bear.

I know it hurts to feel like you're facing the world alone. I know the dull ache of reading poems about the power of friendship and not being able to relate.

But I want you to know that there will come a time when you'll find that person and those words will also make sense to you.

Sometimes, I wish the earth
would stop spinning so I could
step out for a moment—
a fleeting pause in the
ceaseless dance of the
Earth's rotation and
perpetual motion of life.

keep
fighting.

Surviving loss is messy, and that's okay. If you're going through the motions of life after losing someone who once meant everything to you, you have to be gentle with yourself.

Survival isn't a straightforward path; it's a rollercoaster ride of emotions. Some days, you'll wake up feeling hopeful, seeing that flicker of light breaking through the darkness. But other days, the ache of their absence will hit you like a brick wall, leaving you paralyzed with grief.

And you know what? That's okay, too. It's okay to feel lost, to feel broken, to feel everything all at once. Your heart is so much stronger than you think–capable of braving the craziest storms.

But promise yourself this: on your worst days, when the pain feels unbearable and the world seems too heavy to bear, don't give up.

Never ever give up on your worst day.

Hold onto the hope that tomorrow might be a little bit brighter and that healing is not only possible but highly likely.

So, take it one day at a time. Be kind to yourself, and remember that it's okay not to be okay. Reach out to those who love you, lean on them for support, and know that you are never alone in your journey. Never.

Reframe your perception of loneliness. More often than not, you find yourself alone not because you're unlovable but because you prioritized your well-being over comfort. Those long nights confronting the emptiness within are the consequences of tough decisions you had to make. Behind every lonely person lies a story of courage. Be proud of yourself.

By waiting for them to change,
you give them the power to
decide when you can heal.

The only person who can fix
you is you—not the person who
broke you or the one after them.
Only you hold that power.

It's human to feel paralyzed by the what-ifs and the un-knowns, to let the fear of failure hold us back. But the regret of not trying is often far heavier than the fear of failure. When you look back in a few years, what will you see? Will you see a life lived to its fullest, with you going after your dreams, or will you wish you had at least tried?

Don't let anxiety dictate your decisions, and don't let doubt rob you of the chance to grow and succeed. Lean into that discomfort. Acknowledge it, knowing that facing these challenges head-on is the only way to find out just how strong you are.

The road ahead may be long, and there may be many hardships. It's true. However, every step you take, no matter how small, brings you closer to your dreams.

So, please, take the opportunities that come your way despite the fear and doubt. Ultimately, it is not the outcome that defines you but the courage to try. And I promise you, when you look back on this moment years from now, you will be grateful for every risk you took, every dream you chased, and every opportunity you seized.

The most beautiful feeling in the
world is reciprocated love.

It's gazing at someone and knowing
without a doubt that they feel
the same way about you.

It's the simple joy of seeing their name
light up your phone and feeling your
heart skip a beat as anticipation builds.

It's daydreaming about them and wearing
a silly smile on your face all day.

Love is beautiful, and you deserve
a love that's easy and lights up the
darkest corners of your soul.

Don't settle for any less than that.

their
biggest
flaw
was
that
they
weren't
you.

I hope you crash into moments that take your breath away. I hope your mind fills with memories that linger long after they've passed. I hope you find happiness in the quiet moments and laughter in the chaos of every-day life. I hope you discover the beauty in the mundane and the magic in the ordinary.

I hope you learn to love yourself fiercely, quirks and all, and realize that the opinions of others do not determine your worth.

I hope you chase your dreams and never let fear stop you from trying. I hope you find meaning in pursuing your passions and pride in the journey, regardless of the destination.

I hope you don't lose sight of the beauty surrounding you, even in the most challenging times. I hope you find strength in vulnerability and courage in adversity. Above all, I hope you never forget that you are worthy of love, happiness, and all the blessings life offers.

She didn't walk away to
punish him; she walked
away because enduring his
absence was less painful
than living with someone
who didn't respect her.

I hope you meet someone who will notice when you're lost in thoughts and, instead of being upset, will try to understand why you're having an off day.

I hope you meet someone who understands that your quietness is more likely a sign of sadness than anger. I hope you meet someone who acknowledges that there could be countless reasons your head is lost in the clouds. And I hope you find the person to initiate a conversation to understand why you're feeling down rather than reacting angrily.

I hope you find someone who believes the best way to know someone is to understand what makes them sad. I hope you find someone eager to learn what matters to you, your triggers, and how they can better nurture your heart.

Above all, I hope you find someone who understands that some of us crave a hug on rough days while others seek peace. I hope you meet the one who knows that the best way to understand is not to guess but to ask.

you have
it in
you.

You're not asking for too much.

There are people out there who can
give you everything you need.

You've been seeking validation from the wrong
people and it's skewed your perspective.

They took hope from you by walking away
with pieces of your broken heart.

You're not asking for too much.

You're a beautiful human being, both inside and
out. Their inability to recognize your worth says
nothing about you. Absolutely nothing other
than you haven't met the right person yet.

Ah, the bittersweet dance of mixed signals—how frustrating it can be. One moment, they're showering you with attention, lighting up your phone, and always finding a way to cross your path. But the next, they act like a stranger, leaving you to question whether their affection was ever real. They even act distant and aloof, as though the connection you felt was nothing more than a figment of your imagination. You find yourself confused, wondering if you misread their signals or if they're simply playing games.

Here's the truth: they care, but not like you do. They care in their own fleeting way. Their affection comes with conditions and limitations they won't admit to. They're only willing to invest in you when it's convenient and requires minimal effort.

You deserve so much more than half-hearted affection. You deserve someone willing to meet you halfway, who sees your worth and is willing to invest in you entirely. Mixed signals aren't a sign of inner conflict; they reflect someone unwilling to give you the love and respect you deserve.

So don't settle for someone who's only willing to give you half. You deserve a love that's whole, a connection that's genuine. Hold out for someone who's willing to put in the effort, who sees you for the incredible person you are, and who's willing to meet you all the way, not halfway.

There will be moments when you feel like giving up and moments when you feel like you've already given up. But if any part of you still feels that flame, you'll find it in yourself to give it one more shot.

When life gets difficult,
 don't run; draw your sword.

You don't know how strong you
are because you never had to
use your strength to survive.

Strength has always
been within you.

Always.

Listen, you don't need to wait until you've healed to be happy again. Joy can be found in every corner of life. No matter your challenges, you are more than the pain you're experiencing. I'm not suggesting you ignore your pain; it's an essential part of your growth. But I firmly believe that happiness can coexist with pain. Don't postpone happiness until you achieve your dream job, receive a text from your crush, or mend your broken heart. Find happiness in the present moment. Look around you and enjoy what you have rather than what you wish you had.

do
not
settle.

You must forgive yourself for falling for those who couldn't reciprocate your feelings. Forgive yourself for letting your heart lead, sometimes overriding reason. Forgive yourself for disregarding red flags.

When we're in love, we find reasons to overlook what we wouldn't tolerate otherwise. Be proud of how fearlessly you loved, your capacity to forgive, your strength to choose the high road instead of seeking revenge, and your courage not to let pain turn you into someone who hurts others.

Hurt people hurt people, but not you. And that, my friend, is truly something to be proud of.

People are not inherently good or evil.

Good individuals can make bad decisions, and vice versa.

I struggle with this reality not because I question its truth but because it adds complexity to life.

It complicates decision-making.

No definitive numbers or statistics indicate the level of bad choices tolerable in a good person.

Is someone typically good to you deserving of your love if they deeply hurt you once? I don't have the answer.

Often, your heart is the only companion when making decisions that require a clear mind to maintain sanity.

heart
and
mind
often have
opposite
needs,

and neither
is wrong.

Confront your fears.

You won't meet new people if you stay cooped up at home. You won't experience the pride that arises from confronting your anxiety if you don't get out of your comfort zone. You won't feel that overwhelming happiness washing over you when you get an answer from your crush if you don't text them.

Without taking risks, you'll miss out on experiencing new emotions. You might avoid rejection, pain, or failure, but you'll spend a lifetime pondering "what if."

What if you had mustered the courage to give them your number?

What if you had accepted that job offer?

What if you had confronted your fears?

Let me ask you this: what if fear is the only barrier between you and your dreams? What if you simply tried?

Yes, there's a chance of failure. But what if you succeed?

Compassion isn't simply about solving others' problems—it's about acknowledging their feelings. It is understanding someone's distress instead of rushing to find solutions.

I hope you learn to be uncomfortable.

I hope you learn to find value in
the pain, not the suffering itself,
but the lessons it offers.

I hope you come to understand that
discomfort is not synonymous with
failure but a sign that you are growing.

I hope you recognize that challenges
are not just roadblocks but also
opportunities for self-discovery.

I hope you find comfort in knowing
that mistakes are not signs of weakness
but rather badges of courage—proof
that you tried where many gave up.

I hope you view life's challenges
not as insurmountable but as
opportunities to become stronger.

With each setback you overcome, you
emerge stronger and become closer to
the person you were always meant to be.

Anxiety can be paralyzing, and knowing it's here isn't enough to make it disappear. You can't just sweep it away and send it on its way. It has a mind of its own.

Anxiety is that nagging voice in your head whispering that you're not good enough, not pretty enough, not smart enough. It dictates every move you make, or rather, don't make. It's the voice in your head urging you to remain in your comfort zone.

Anxiety is that monologue that emanates from within, attempting to shield you, albeit poorly. Anxiety is an overprotective friend that doesn't know boundaries.

But anxiety isn't truly you.

One day, you'll realize that you have the power to silence that voice. It won't happen overnight, and it won't be easy, but as impossible as it seems today, it won't always feel that way.

Anxiety is the only thing standing between you and your dreams.

You got this. Truly.

your
fear
wants you
to believe
it's a
lost cause,
but that's
a lie.

there is
always hope.

you
are not
alone.

It's ironic, isn't it? We invest so much effort into connecting with others, yet we shy away from sharing what truly makes us human: our emotions.

There's this strange modesty around feelings. Why do we feel shame about experiencing sadness, anger, or distress? Why is vulnerability perceived as weakness?

Though the world sometimes feels like a jungle, we do not need to pretend to be strong to survive. Sharing our emotions allows us to forge connections, alleviating that sense of solitude. We aren't meant to endure loneliness indefinitely; we're meant to connect.

So, here's my plea to you: open up. Send that text message and post that heartfelt Instagram post. Tell your mom you love her. Be real. Be vulnerable.

Life is filled with contrasts—ups
and downs, highs and lows.

Just remember that whatever you're
feeling right now is temporary.

The light at the end of the tunnel
may seem distant, but each day you
fight, you are getting closer to it.

I promise the light is there even if
you can't see it. Hold on to that.

It's true that sometimes, following your heart can make you lose your mind, but following your mind can also break your heart.

We're told that the right thing to do is to follow our minds because our minds reason. But who are we to decide that rational thinking is always the best decision?

When I look back at the best moments of my life, they were often preceded by choices made from the heart, choices made against people's best advice.

Making decisions based on the heart's desires won't always pay off, but we shouldn't be so quick to dismiss our feelings to follow our rational thoughts.

My mind often tricks me. It's the first to run me through worst-case scenarios and remind me why I shouldn't pursue my dreams. It's skilled at recalling instances of failure and the pain of heartbreak.

My mind is overprotective. It has good intentions but its constant control of what I should or shouldn't do often leads to more sadness.

My mind tends to be too negative and rational, while my heart is the eternal optimist.

It's another way life puts contrasts into us.

Happiness lies in the balance.

You can't force something into your life. If something is right, you'll never have to wonder. You won't feel lost; you won't feel conflicted. What is right for you will stay. You won't have to chase it; you won't have to mend it. You won't have to bend backward to make it fit your life. When something is right for you, it will bring you peace.

There was a reason for those pieces that so painfully didn't fit into your life. There's *always* a reason. I promise you, one day, you will be thankful that the very same thing you wished so hard to have in your life didn't work out.

you can't
fix every
broken soul
you come
in contact
with.

I hope you don't let life harden
you after another heartbreak.

I hope you don't convince yourself you are
unworthy of love because of your mistakes.

I hope you learn to forgive yourself
when the weight of regrets steals
another night of sleep away from you.

I hope you allow people to love you, no
matter how low your self-confidence is.

But above all, I hope you realize you
are worth more than your fears and
insecurities. I hope you start believing
in your true potential and realize that
the only thing standing between you and
your dreams is you. It's always been you.

Sometimes, the most helpful
thing you can do is to do nothing
at all. Instead, take a moment.

Allow yourself to sit with your
emotions before jumping into action.
Understand what just happened before
making any life-changing decisions.

Sometimes, the kindest thing
you can do for yourself is to sit
still in the whirlwind of life.

trust
that loss
steered you
in the
right
direction.

The fear of failure and suffering can often be more daunting than the actual experience itself. Anxiety has a way of holding us back.

Instead of imagining achieving your goal, try picturing failure. Imagine the worst-case scenario. It may feel counterintuitive, but try it.

What if you're on stage, ready to deliver a speech, and suddenly your mind goes blank? What if tears start flowing uncontrollably? What if you collapse from the stress? What might happen?

You might feel disappointed or ashamed, but the audience will not perceive that. They'll witness someone who courageously stepped out of their comfort zone and tried—and that's what you should see, too!

What if you gave that person your number and they didn't call you? Then what? It's sad; allow yourself to feel that, but remember, just because someone doesn't reciprocate your feelings doesn't mean the next person won't appreciate you. And don't forget about all the people who wish they had your number whom you may not have met yet.

What else are you afraid of? Imagine your worst-case scenario. Then, find a way to fight back against your negative thoughts.

If you fail, you'll be somewhat prepared. But if you don't, ah, that victory has the potential to become a core memory.

When you need it most, you'll realize just how strong you are—tapping into a well of strength you didn't know you had.

Sometimes, staying becomes
an act of defiance against the
fears that echo in your mind.
It's a silent rebellion against the
expected norm. Most people
would leave, it's true, but you're
not one to give in to external
pressures. That's your strength.

I'm sorry you never got the apology you deserved. It's a shame they had enough courage to hurt you but not enough to acknowledge the consequences. The good news is that you don't need them to heal. True healing comes from within–you have the power to heal yourself.

when
love
becomes
challenging,
don't act
impulsively.

sit still.

Her strong sense of independence
is a product of consistent letdowns.
By taking matters into her own
hands and not relying on others,
she's protecting herself against
expected disappointment.

I wish we could redefine success.
"34-year-old woman got up this
morning despite another heartbreak,"
may not make headlines, but it should.
Let's normalize those mundane
victories that make us human, no
matter how ordinary they appear.

Someday, when you least expect it, that weight you've been carrying will start to lift.

Your mind and heart will align, and you'll be filled with newfound hope. You'll feel a sudden rush to step out into the world, leaving your comfort zone far behind.

And that's precisely what you'll do.

Ten things that make you human:

1. *making mistakes.*

2. *changing your mind.*

3. *getting angry at people you love.*

4. *crying.*

5. *having ups and downs.*

6. *not always being the best version of yourself.*

7. *feeling lost.*

8. *being unproductive.*

9. *wishing you had done something differently.*

10. *needing to be alone.*

Be brave enough to accept
being disliked. Do what your
heart tells you, not to please
others or fit in, but because
it sets your soul on fire.

Dear ten-year-old me,

First and foremost, I want you to know how incredibly proud I am of you for bravely navigating through all the challenges life has thrown your way. There were countless moments when you could have given up, but you persevered. Every challenge became a lesson learned, and I wouldn't be who I am today without your resilience. So, thank you.

I understand that life has hurt you deeply. People have let you down, and you're wondering why they had to leave. To you, it seemed obvious they had a choice, but adults always find ways to justify their departures.

I know how tough it is being a kid and feeling like you have no control over the unfolding events in your life. Right now, there's a lot of pain, and it's confusing. Please know that you haven't done anything wrong. Sometimes, even good people find themselves in situations entirely beyond their control. It's tough and it's unfair. But you may not realize that everything you're experiencing is shaping you into the incredible person you are destined to become.

Every painful moment is a lesson in disguise. I'm sorry you have to learn these lessons at such a young age, but they're shaping you into the person you were always meant to become. Your journey won't always unfold exactly as you envisioned, but what I admire most about you is that you never give up. You'll encounter plenty of obstacles along the way but you'll always find the strength to overcome them.

Your resilience will leave people in awe. And you know who will be the most impressed? Me.

I'm immensely proud of you. When I think back to the little girl you were, pouring your heart out onto paper, seeking comfort in a fort made of pillows and sheets, it makes my heart happy.

Life dealt you a tough hand but you turned it into a winning hand through your strength and determination.

You might wonder if your dreams will ever come true. I can't speak for all of them yet, but many will.

So, hang in there, little one. Even though your dreams may take a different shape than you imagined, I promise you will reach them. They might even surpass your expectations. You're destined for greatness.

With love and admiration,

Your older self

i hope you
surround
yourself
with people
who will
have your back
when you're not
in the
room.

The more you confront your fears, the more they lose their hold. At first, challenges will appear at every turn, making you question your decision to step out of your comfort zone. But this is where your strength comes in; it will become easier if you persist and keep trying despite imperfect experiences.

It may seem counterintuitive, but the more you familiarize yourself with setbacks, the less daunting they become. It's not about getting used to discomfort but developing strategies to overcome it.

The day you face something that truly terrifies you and know you'll be okay no matter what is when you realize you've made it. You've conquered your anxiety and become stronger than that nagging voice in your head.

the
ultimate
failure
is letting
fear of
failure
stop you
from
trying.

You've grown so used to people treating you poorly that your mind expects nothing more than the bare minimum. So when someone goes above and beyond for you out of genuine care, they win your heart instantly. There's beauty in that but be careful not to mistake common human decency with love.

she's
broken
but
too afraid
to ask
for help.

There's something bittersweet about independence born from constant letdowns. It's not a choice—it's survival. It's doing everything yourself because you know it won't get done if you don't. It's refraining from asking for help because you anticipate being let down. It's venturing out alone because you expect silence if you reach out.

The independence gained from enduring a cycle of disappointment is both a curse and a blessing. It's a valuable skill but also a reminder of the challenges you've had to face. If you're one of those independent people, I see you. I know what it takes for you to keep showing up when the world hasn't been kind to you. Be proud of yourself.

don't
forget
that there
is a lesson
behind
every
setback.

Try one more time. If it doesn't
work out, try again, and then
once more. The difference
between success and failure is
that some people stop trying.

When someone rejects you, they only dismiss one facet of who you are. The irony is that what one person rejects you for could be what makes the next fall in love with you.

Remember how, at the peak of your confidence, you took on challenges that seemed out of your league.

Yet your assurance was so undeniable that nobody questioned you. Some call this 'blissful ignorance'; I call it confidence.

What's crazy is that if you gave me a chance to change the past and not endure all the suffering I went through, I probably wouldn't take you up on the offer. All those days spent in the dark, not knowing how I would dig myself out of the hole, shaped me into who I am today. If it weren't for all the pain I've been through, I wouldn't be as resilient. Pain is a strict but effective teacher.

If you're facing something impossible right now and wondering if happiness is still possible, let me assure you it is. It might take time, but you'll find the strongest version of yourself at the end of that long tunnel. That person is you. You're becoming right now. Trust the process. Despite the contradiction, pain is healing you.

I know there are some endings in your life that you wish you could rewrite, moments where you wish things had turned out differently. But if you were to rewrite those endings, you wouldn't be the person you are today.

Each experience, whether happy or painful, shaped you into who you are. Don't dwell on what could have been, be proud of who you've become, thanks to those endings.

Never give anyone the impression that you dug yourself out of the dark for them. Your comeback isn't about proving anything to anyone else. It's not about seeking validation from those who broke you. No, that victory is for you and you alone. It's an apology to yourself.

So, don't cheapen that win by pretending it was all for someone else. No, it was a battle fought and won from within. It was a promise to yourself that you would never again allow another human being to dictate your destiny.

Your journey and your victories belong to you. Don't let anyone minimize your achievements or belittle your struggles. Own them—they are the heart of your story.

Here's to you, the battles you've fought and the mountains you've climbed. Always remember that your strength lies not in the validation of those who couldn't love you but in your confidence.

Pain doesn't erase the happy parts of you. It buries them deep. It takes effort to dig yourself out when more keeps adding up. But beneath the pain, you are alive–the more you push back, the stronger that inner strength grows. Keep fighting to reclaim that fire that used to be yours. It's buried under pain but it's still there, waiting for you to nurse that flame back to life. It's still there.

don't
give your
whole
to someone
only capable
of offering
half.

You don't have to hate them or regret the entire relationship just because it ended. Your heart doesn't have to be remorseful because they broke your trust. The happy times still matter, even if things don't work out.

You can still be thankful for the good times. There was a time when it was just you and them against the world, and even though love changes, it doesn't take away the past. Don't grow bitter; don't let the end of a relationship rewrite what was once very real. Move forward without letting hate win.

stop
making
excuses
for them.

trust them
the first time
they reveal
their true
nature.

If you decide to stay, don't do it hoping to change them. Meaningful and lasting change only comes from within. They need to want that change for themselves. Not for you. Only stay if you love them for who they are, not for who you hope they'll become.

the best
advice
I was ever
given
is to not
fall in love
with
potential.

You didn't think you could survive
another heartbreak,

And yet, here you are.

You didn't think you could step out
of your comfort zone again,

And yet, here you are.

You didn't think you'd survive that
brutal chapter of your life,

And yet, here you are.

You didn't think you'd ever rise above adversity,

And yet, here you are.

Life may have thrown you many obstacles,
and you may have tripped over them, but you
never gave up. You learned how to get back up.

When times get tough, remember those
moments when you felt like there was
no end in sight. Remember those days
and tell yourself: "Yet, here I am."

You need to let go of things that
were never meant to be yours.
Sometimes, what you perceive as
the universe being harsh on you is
instead the universe sending you
a message. It's telling you to let go
before becoming too deeply invested.

Here's a hard truth: no matter how much you love someone, they may not find a permanent place in your heart. Many of those we form deep connections with only pass through for a short chapter. Yet, there's a certain beauty in these short connections.

We tend to spend energy trying to force relationships into our lives instead of moving on. It's painful when those we thought would always be by our side leave, yet there's always a lesson to be learned. Finding wisdom in the middle of the pain might take time, but it's always worth it.

As difficult as it is, try to appreciate the beauty of those temporary connections and the lessons they bring.

just
because
you stumbled
today
doesn't mean
you'll fall
tomorrow.

It's okay to gaze into the mirror and not recognize the person who looked back at you yesterday. It's okay to feel disconnected from your past self. It's okay to feel lost sometimes. None of us have it all figured out. We stumble, we fall, we learn. That's how we evolve.

Please don't be ashamed of actions you took yesterday that you wouldn't take today. Remember that a few decades ago, people smoked on planes and car seats were considered a luxury.

People learn. People change. People evolve.

The past, present, and future versions of yourself are all chapters of your story. They're different versions of you, but they're still you. Those early chapters are an essential part of your story, shaping you. Be kind to yourself. Growth is messy but it's truly beautiful.

People throw words on paper as if reading them made them an easy task. You'll often hear "just ignore," or "just block them," or "just leave." *Just…*

It's as if it were an easy decision, as if no feelings were involved. It's as if all you have to do is look at the situation rationally, poll people around you, and follow the majority. I wish things were this black and white, but they're often not.

"Just ignore" is not easy when someone unfairly pushes all your buttons. Those words are dismissive, as if the complexity of human emotions could simply be swept aside with a simple command. But it's never as simple as flipping a switch. How do you ignore the pounding of your heart, the knot in your stomach, when every word, every gesture, feels like a direct assault on your soul? It takes strength, a strength that goes beyond willpower. It takes resilience, it takes patience, and, above all, it takes self-love.

And then there's "just block them," as if pressing a button could erase someone from your life as quickly as clearing your browser history. But what about the memories, the shared moments, the laughter and the tears? How do you simply delete a chapter of your story, pretending it never existed? It's not about blocking them from your feed; it's about washing them off the very fabric of your being.

Finally, the radical option: "Just leave." Oh, if only it were that easy. If only you could simply sever ties with someone who once held your heart in their hand. But what about the vows you exchanged, the promises whispered in the dead of night? What about the dreams you built together, the future you planned? Separation isn't just a legal process; it's a rebuilding of the soul, a tearing apart of two lives that have lived together for years.

So the next time someone tells you to "just" do something, take a moment to pause, to breathe, and to honor the complexity of your emotions. Life is messy, beautiful, and chaotic, and it's rarely as simple as a single word or action. It's complex, and we, as humans, need to understand and appreciate its complexity.

If someone genuinely wants a forever home in your heart, they'll find their way without you chasing after them. When it's right, there's an effortless ease. When it's right, you know.

sometimes,
failure
is a form
of resilience—

a stubborn
refusal to
stay down.

It's okay to fall. You may get up a little bruised but it won't kill you. Yes, failing hurts. It stings like nothing else but it's a great teacher and reminder that you are human.

After all, we're all experiencing life for the first time and learning as we go. In that shared struggle, there's beauty, hope, and the promise of a brighter tomorrow, no matter how many times we may fall.

which
do you
believe
hurts more:

the sting
of failure
or the ache
of regret?

I know life hasn't always been kind to you.

I know you've been through more than your fair share of pain and I know the marks it's left on your soul. But I hope you haven't let those scars convince you that there's no good left in the world.

Despite all the darkness you've experienced, there is still light within you and everywhere. That spark of hope that refuses to be shut down is proof of your bravery—a reminder that you can find happiness no matter how many times life knocks you down.

There may be moments when the weight of the world is crushing you but please, don't forget that happiness is there, waiting for you. You are worthy of love, joy, and all the beautiful things life has to offer. So keep holding on. Hang on tight.

no matter
how often
life knocks
her down,

she always
finds a way
to get
back up.

Your worth does not depend on how successful you are. And I don't just mean how successful you are in achieving your dreams; I mean how successful you are in leaving your comfort zone.

Sometimes, no matter how hard you try, you won't be able to get yourself out of the dark at a particular moment, but that does not mean that you are less than. It just means that it's not the right time for you. Sometimes, waking up in the morning and not giving up is the bravest thing you can do. That's success.

sometimes,
the hardest
decision
isn't to leave.

it's to stay.

You often learn more from the moments in your life that tear you apart than from those that pass through you like a breeze.

You learn more from moments that show you how not to love rather than how to. There is wisdom in the ache. Through tears shed and healed wounds, you will learn what it truly means to be human and vulnerable. You will learn to fall in love with pieces of yourself that you never liked before.

Adversity is how you build character; that's how your strength is tested. Trust me, it's in the depths of sadness that you'll discover that strength was always within you. Always.

So, embrace the pain, the heartache, and all those moments that threaten to tear you apart. They are the catalysts you need to grow, learn, and evolve. Every setback is a lesson in disguise.

Trust in your resilience and know that every moment, whether painful or joyful, is shaping you into the person you were always meant to be.

Happiness truly starts with you. If you keep relying on others to make you happy, you'll be disappointed time and time again. You have to learn how to fill that void within yourself without depending on anyone else. Learn to love yourself. Learn to be uncomfortable. Learn to be okay with solitude. Everything else that comes your way is just a bonus—it's all about finding that inner peace first.

remember
when you
felt like you'd
never be
happy again...

and now
remember
when you felt
happy again.

You may be sad about that door
closing today, but down the road,
you'll wish you had just nailed
that door shut from the start
instead of trying to keep it open.

it's okay
to be lost.

In moments of confusion, it can be hard to differentiate between love and comfort, between the fear of being alone and the need to forgive, between something you genuinely desire and have been misled into thinking you want.

You may believe you love them even though they broke your heart. But if you can feel this deeply for someone who caused so much pain, just imagine the love you'll be capable of for the right person. Imagine what it will feel like to meet someone who knows how to love you effortlessly—every single part of you.

As much as I want you to
understand that healing is
ultimately your responsibility,
I also want you to know that you
don't have to go through it alone.

Dear partner,

I'm sorry for not always being the best version of myself.

I'm sorry for sometimes prioritizing winning an argument over finding common ground. At times, I get so caught up in winning arguments that I forget it's not about being right; it's about being together.

I'm sorry for forgetting my own advice and only turning to you when I have a page-long to-do list.

I'm sorry for not doing my part in keeping that spark alive. For being too busy. Too proud. Too me.

It's difficult to admit you've been wrong, but I'm here doing just that. I've let my ego get in the way, prioritizing winning over understanding.

I miss those moments when it felt like we were truly in sync, when just being together was enough. Life gets busy, I get it, but that's no excuse for letting our connection fade. So, I'm sorry for not doing my part to keep the flame alive.

But I don't want my words to be just words. Let's make time for us for the things that matter most. Let's laugh, let's talk, and let's rediscover what made us fall in love. Because it's not about being perfect; it's about being there for each other, flaws and all—for better and worse.

You need to heal yourself, not because you're trying to win someone back or seek external validation; you need to want it because it's what's best for you. But that doesn't mean you can't lean on others for support; you should. If people offer you a hand to hold or a shoulder to cry on, take it. They may not be able to heal you or take away all your pain but they can be there for you while you heal yourself. Don't shut yourself off from the world and don't let it harden you. Keep letting people in. Let them help you while you help yourself.

Please, do not wait for life
to be *easy* to start being
happy. You can't wait until
your life is perfect in every
shape and form to allow your
heart to feel light again.

Life has no easy answers; there will never be a one-size-fits-all approach. That's why you're bound to stumble at times, why you need to be comfortable with failure, and why you need to be open to learning and growing.

There is no definitive guidebook to life, at least not one that guarantees success. What works for one person may not work for you and that's okay. You have to make your own mistakes and learn from them.

Happiness is built over time through hard work, tears, and experience. You can have a high-paying job, a loving partner, and friends and yet still feel empty. On the other hand, you can be happy living paycheck to paycheck, with only yourself as a companion.

Happiness isn't easy to achieve, but there's one sure thing: it's not attained by working tirelessly at a job you hate to reach what looks good on a resume or what will impress your Instagram followers.

Happiness starts in your heart. It's about finding that thing that makes you want to cry because it feels so good. It is being content with where you are and where you're going. It's about what you *are* bringing to the world rather than what you *could* be doing. Happiness is subjective and can be challenging in a world where appearances are so important.

If you find yourself in the dark, I hope you know that it does not reflect your worth, but above all, I hope you know that you can be happy again.

Many of us have gone through challenges we thought we'd never overcome. We don't post about them on social media because it's not as glamorous as a selfie in front of the Eiffel Tower.

Yet, we've dug ourselves out of the dark, and you can too. You are stronger than that voice trying to convince you you are worthless. You get to decide what makes you happy. You get to define success.

You can build your happiness again, piece by piece. Whatever happiness means to you, do that thing and build from there. Take a walk, sip a fancy cappuccino at the coffee shop, and look at the sky. Buy that over-priced sweatshirt. Reach out to an old friend. Stare at the stars. Find happiness in the little things, for they've always been the big things and add up fast.

She tried to forget him with someone else to mend her broken heart. He was everything she needed—everything she ever wanted in a partner. He told her 'I love you' daily. He made her feel like she was the center of his universe. He made her feel seen and safe. He loved her more than she ever loved herself, which is precisely why it failed. True happiness with someone else is difficult until you've mastered self-love.

Be kind to yourself in moments of anxiety. No matter how irrational your fears may seem, your mind perceives them as real. You're not overreacting, and you're not broken or a lost cause.

You're not a failure because you can't control your panic. Your past experiences left marks—your mind is simply trying to protect you. Please, don't get mad at those parts of yourself that don't yet know how to ground you gently. They're doing their best.

There will come a time when you can calmly reassure your mind that your worst fears won't come true. But for now, it's okay not to be there yet. It's okay.

You may feel confident about your decision today, only to wake up uncertain tomorrow. There are moments in life when we think we finally see clearly, only to realize that a moment of clarity isn't necessarily the correct answer in the long term.

Sometimes, the right decision on paper
differs from the right in real life.

Sometimes, the right decision
for a night isn't forever.

Sometimes, today's great decision
isn't tomorrow's best decision.

There often isn't a universal right or wrong answer.

Be kind to yourself in those moments
of contradiction. Believe me, you're not
losing your mind; you're just human.

If you've just discovered that the person you share a life with had an affair, you need to be gentle with yourself.

Give yourself permission to feel it all. Scream if you must, cry if you need to—let it all out.

But remember that while allowing yourself to feel all the feels is important, it is equally necessary to prevent them from overwhelming your entire being. Believe me, I know that it's one of the most challenging things you'll ever do. But you owe it to yourself to release the grip of anger as soon as possible.

I know how shocking it is to realize that your mind and body are even capable of feeling such intense negative emotions but please, don't let them consume you. Take control of them.

Remind yourself that you are strong—so much stronger than you think you are. Use those emotions as a source of empowerment and let them become the fuel that propels you forward. Let them ignite a fire within you—one that can't be extinguished. Ask yourself: What have you always dreamed of doing but have yet to pursue? What passions have you been putting aside? And pursue those. Negative emotions can be used as a motivator. Use them.

Finally, remember that pain, as excruciating as it may be, is temporary and also a great teacher. So, let it guide you.

Humans are chameleons. We constantly adapt to the people we're with and our environments. Your banker knows a version of yourself that your best friend doesn't, and vice versa.

Some people will only ever get to see one version of you, and perhaps that version they see isn't something they like. I know it's painful to ponder the other versions of yourself they might have loved, but ultimately, you must understand that the only version of you that matters is the one you are with yourself, the one you are behind closed doors when no one is watching. If you love that person, then you've won in life.

In a world where hearts are often bruised by others' self-interest, it's easy to lose sight of our worthiness.

No matter how often you've been let down, betrayed, or deeply wounded, I promise you that you are worthy.

Love is not reserved for those with an unbroken heart. There are people out there who will love you just as you are—broken pieces and all. They will love every piece of you, even those parts you try so hard to bury.

Shut down that little voice of insecurities in your head and instead open your heart to the possibility of love.

Because you are worthy of love no matter how many times your heart has been broken, how many tears you've shed, or how many scars you carry. Don't you forget it.

We convince ourselves we're not good enough—that we don't deserve any better. We fool ourselves into thinking we're stuck. But happiness isn't found in our comfort zones. No. It's found in the courage to confront the unknown. It's found in the realization that the only thing stopping us is our fear. So stand up for yourself and for your happiness. Life is too short to settle.

If you find yourself constantly censoring your thoughts and actions just to be the person you think they want you to be, they're not right for you.

If they disappear when life gets tough, leaving you alone to face life's challenges, they're not right for you.

If every conversation feels like a performance rather than a spontaneous and genuine connection, they're not right for you.

If they prioritize their needs above yours, never considering your feelings, they're not right for you.

If you feel like you're walking on eggshells, afraid to speak your mind for fear of their reaction, they're not right for you.

If being with them drains your energy rather than replenishing it, they're not right for you.

If you constantly question where you stand with them, unsure of their feelings towards you, they're not right for you.

If they make you feel small, insignificant, or unworthy, they're not right for you.

If being around them brings out the worst in you rather than the best, they're not right for you.

If they don't celebrate your successes or support your dreams, they're not right for you.

If they try to change you, criticizing what makes you who you are, they're not right for you.

If they only love the idea of you, not the reality, they're not right for you.

If they don't make you feel loved, cherished, and valued every single day, they're not right for you.

Because if you can't be yourself around them, if they only show up on your good days, if you're always the one initiating, they're not right for you.

When your intuition whispers doubts in your mind, listen to it. It knows when something isn't right for you.

With billions of people in this world, don't stay in a relationship because you're afraid of the unknown. Don't close yourself off to meeting the one who is right for you by trying to force a relationship that was never meant to work. Open up.

and
yet–

here
you
are

You may not have expected to reach the
end of this book. And yet, here you are.

Thank you for being open to vulnerability.

Thank you for sharing this
human experience with me.

Thank you for indulging in the
power of contradiction.

I hope this book made you feel
less alone in your journey.

With love and much understanding,

Eileen

ABOUT THE AUTHOR

Eileen Lamb, the heart and soul behind The Autism Cafe, is the author of *All Across The Spectrum* and *Be The One*. A French native turned Texan, she's not just an author but a mom, photographer, public speaker, and podcast host. Alongside her sons, Charlie and Jude, and their sister, Billie, Eileen's journey is about connecting with others through vulnerability and authenticity. Her writing isn't just words on a page—it's a hug and a shoulder to lean on. Eileen is on a mission to ensure no one feels alone, and she's doing it with a lot of heart.

INSTAGRAM | @inkwellcafe

MORE FROM
THOUGHT CATALOG BOOKS

Books by Eileen Lamb

Be The One

All Across the Spectrum

You might also like

When You're Ready, This Is How You Heal
by Brianna Wiest

You're Overthinking It:
Find Lifelong Love By Being Your True Self
by Sabrina Alexis Bendory

Eyes On The Road
by Michell C. Clark

Anticipate Good Things Coming
by Stephanie Fonseca

Moments To Hold Close
by Molly Burford

Holding Space for the Sun
by Jamal Cadoura

**THOUGHT
CATALOG**
Books

THOUGHTCATALOG.COM